Uncle Gary & Aunt Sylvia,

Thank you for letting us stay with you. You two are very kind and generous.

We love this book and re-read chapters often. We hope you enjoy it, too.

THE *Unexpected* DELIVERER

Love,

Steve, Marybeth, and Christina

April 29, 2021

THE *Unexpected* DELIVERER

EMILY BELLE FREEMAN
DAVID BUTLER

DESERET
BOOK

Library of Congress Cataloging-in-Publication Data

Names: Freeman, Emily, 1969– author. | Butler, David, author.
Title: The unexpected Deliverer / Emily Belle Freeman, David Butler.
 Description: Salt Lake City, Utah : Deseret Book, [2021] | Includes bibliographical references. | Summary: "Jesus is our Redeemer, our Deliverer from sin and death. But His deliverance often comes in unexpected ways. This inspirational book examines several events in the Lord's ministry (including His premortal and postmortal roles) and shows how we can find hope in His promises"—Provided by publisher.
Identifiers: LCCN 2020043126 | ISBN 9781629728773 (trade paperback)
Subjects: LCSH: Jesus Christ—Mormon interpretations. | Jesus Christ—Biography. | The Church of Jesus Christ of Latter-day Saints—Doctrines. | Mormon Church—Doctrines.
Classification: LCC BX8643.J4 F738 2021 | DDC 232.088/2893—dc23
LC record available at https://lccn.loc.gov/2020043126

Printed in the United States of America
Publishers Printing, Salt Lake City, UT

10   9   8   7   6   5   4   3   2   1

For Cade:

This is the friend I've been telling you about.
I think you are going to love Him.

—EBF

For Jeff and Suz,

who love like He does.

—DB

Contents

"...AND THOU SHALT CALL
HIS NAME *Jesus*..."

—Matthew 1:21

HEBREW:

יְשׁוּעַ

Y'SHUA

MEANING:
TO DELIVER; TO RESCUE

Before

Thousands of years before the holy baby was even born in the stable, the Jehovah of the Old Testament, *Jesus,* lived and moved among His people.

He was given the name *Jesus* not only because of what He would do but because of who He already was.

The Deliverer.

When His people found themselves in an impossible situation, Jehovah wasn't just a bystander. Each individual story, as well as the collection of them all, reveals Him as the Deliverer. But oftentimes His deliverance looked different from what you might expect.

He was a rescuer who entered ordinary stories in the most unlikely ways.

Perhaps you think your story is ordinary. Maybe it feels

unfixable. You might think the time for deliverance has passed.

You're not alone.

When Isaac started up Mount Moriah with his father and a pile of wood, he didn't know about the ram caught in the thicket. When they came to the place God told them to go, when his father built an altar there and laid the wood in order and bound Isaac upon the wood, the situation seemed unfixable.

But Isaac didn't know about the ram.

He wouldn't find out until Abraham stretched forth his hand and raised the knife—in the very moment when the angel called out of heaven to *stop*. It was such unexpected timing.

And how did that ram get caught in the thicket?

Then Abraham named that place *Jehovah-jireh,* meaning, "the Lord will see and provide" (see Genesis 22:14). Even if the seeing and providing looked different from what was expected.

Isaac's story is not the only one. Right from the start of the Old Testament, we see the Deliverer working in unexpected ways—architecting an ark on behalf of a man who wasn't a shipbuilder (see Genesis 6–9) and providing a well in a desert place for a woman and her son (see Genesis 21:8–21).

But that isn't all. Who would have thought a boy thrown in a pit, sold as a slave, then cast into prison—a dreamer—would become second to Pharaoh? What were the odds that a younger brother with a fancy coat would somehow become the means of saving an entire nation? (see Genesis 35–50).

A nation that wasn't even his own.

We notice Him again on the banks of the Red Sea, as if the ten plagues and the red sacrifice painted on the doorposts were not surprising enough. When the children of Israel looked out over the expanse of water, did they wonder if the Lord had already exhausted all of His miracles on their behalf? Now the army raged behind and the sea stood in front, and how would Jehovah see and provide?

"Stand still," Moses said, "and see the salvation of the Lord. . . . The Lord shall fight for you" (Exodus 14:13–14)—and Moses stretched out his hand. Then the strong east wind started to blow. That wind blew all night until the land was dry, until they could walk through the middle of the sea on dry ground.

No one had walked through a sea before.

And no one had ever taken down an entire enemy city with a lantern, a trumpet, and a pitcher, but Gideon did. He defeated an army of 135,000 with 300 men. They stood every man in his place and blew the trumpets and shattered the pitchers, and the light shone, and the soldiers shouted, "The sword of the Lord, and of Gideon" (Judges 7:20).

Cities aren't usually conquered with shattered pitchers.

What about the shepherd boy with his stone? On that day, in the middle of two large armies, it took only one stone out of five to kill the giant. Goliath came with a sword and a spear and a shield, but David came in the name of the Lord of Hosts. It is another reminder: when the battle is the Lord's, you should expect the unexpected (see 1 Samuel 17).

Everyone knows battles aren't won with one stone.

Consider this. When an entire people are about to be slaughtered, who chooses a woman to overthrow the decree? Especially in a society where women are looked down upon. But a woman would rise to the occasion, a woman who had been put in place for such a time as this (see Esther 4). Who raises up a woman for such a task?

The Lord does.

He is the One who stood with Shadrach, Meshach, and Abed-nego in a furnace with fire too hot to survive. Seven times too hot. It was a death sentence ordered for their defiance to bow down to the king's idols—the king who questioned, "Who is that God that shall deliver you out of my hands?" (Daniel 3:15) and then wondered why there were four men in the fiery furnace instead of three.

"*. . . and the form of the fourth was like the Son of God . . .*" (Daniel 3:25).

The same God who saw the man praying in his chamber in secret, who watched that same man get thrown into a den of lions, who surely looked down and noted the fast of a king who rose very early in the morning and went in haste to the place. Can you imagine that king standing outside that den and crying, "O Daniel, servant of the living God, is thy God, whom thou servest continually, able to deliver thee from the lions?" (Daniel 6:20).

When Daniel answered back from inside the den, the king knew.

Daniel's God was a God of unexpected deliverance.

"So Daniel was taken up out of the den, and no

manner of hurt was found upon him, because he believed in his God" (Daniel 6:23).

This is the God we believe in. The God of rams in thickets. The shipbuilder, the well giver, the prison breaker. A God who opens up seas and dries up mud. The One who wins battles with broken pitchers and single stones, who stands in fiery furnaces and closes the mouths of lions. Every story is different, but the outcome is the same.

Unexpected deliverance.

What about your story?

Where is your fiery furnace, your raging battle, your desert place?

"Is any thing too hard for the Lord?" (Genesis 18:14).

You might think your story
is unfixable, unredeemable,
beyond expectation.

That just means He might not
come as you expect Him to.

But He will come.

The Beginning

LUKE 2

It wasn't what it should have been.

Usually royalty makes quite an impressive entrance. Blaring trumpets. Banner-clad balconies. Dazzling processions.

For the birth of the King of Kings, you might have thought an elegant gala would have been arranged. Majesty greeted by dignitaries. Gilded invitations. Pomp and circumstance.

But not this king.

It was a silent night that followed a restless and unsettling day. The woman's constant pain caused an urgency to find shelter, and yet they were turned away—unwelcome in every place. It wasn't what they expected. Did they hold on to what should have been? Where they should have been? How things should have been? At what point did they let those things go?

At what point would you?

If we hold on too tightly to what should have been, we will miss what God is doing where we are.

One night, great joy showed up in a stable. It was a place of filth, a place no one would choose to be; it was off the beaten path. But He still came. Sometimes what feels like an accidental place is a destination divinely orchestrated by God.

He was her firstborn. Perhaps, like most new mothers, Mary had envisioned how it would be: a clean room, a soft bed, a quiet space with Joseph. But that wasn't true in this case. Instead of a birth behind closed doors, private and intimate, with clean linens and swept floors, this birth happened amidst dung and debris in a space that was unwanted and unfamiliar. And yet, the Jesus we meet in the stable begins His life with an invitation: visitors welcome.

He is the welcoming in.

The door was open from the very beginning. None were turned away, not even strangers. Even in the dung and debris, even in the place filled with mess and unfamiliarity, He welcomed the arrival of kings and paupers—both extremes and everyone in between. With Him, rustic became holy, the lowly became exalted, the royal became reverent in awe.

Come, the stable whispered, *see what God is doing here.*

Even though you would not expect to find Him in this place.

Even though everything says it shouldn't be so.

This is the unexpected beginning of a king.

It is a story that reminds us not to be afraid of stable places or dark but starlit journeys.

Not to hold on to what should have been—the way things should have been.

To start looking instead for the unanticipated. The surprising. The impossible.

It is the message you will find written throughout His life, in His miracles, in His atoning death, and in the prophecies that surround His coming again. The New Testament is filled with these unexpected moments. They take place while He is sitting next to a well, walking on water, eating with sinners, touching a leper, forgiving an adulteress, and conversing with a criminal on a cross.

Unexpected moments that all began with the unlikely circumstances of His birth.

Why would you not find those unexpected moments in your own life?

The unimaginable.

In places of disappointment, we should remember that God visits stables. Even unwanted destinations can become holy with Him. Maybe, when something doesn't make sense, it is time to look for hope in unlikely places. Often it is in the unexpected that the character of Christ is manifest.

If you find yourself holding on to
what should have been,
you might be missing

the *unanticipated,*

the *surprising,*

the *impossible*

right where you are.

The People

JOHN 4

Most Jews walked around it entirely.

Not because that was easier—it actually added two days to the journey. It was because they considered the people traitors, second-class citizens, unclean. Less. The rift had gone on for centuries. They despised the people there. So, Jews didn't walk through Samaria.[1]

But Jesus did.

" . . . he *must needs go* through Samaria" (John 4:4; emphasis added).

Where might He must needs go for you?

The disciples must have questioned why. It really was so unexpected.

But they followed, and when they arrived in Samaria, they left Him sitting by a well and went to buy food. It was the well outside the city, the one used by the outcasts.

Jacob's Well. Jesus waited there in the heat of the day, the sixth hour, the time no one visited wells. He had nothing to draw up water with.[2]

Until she came.

"Give me to drink" (John 4:7). The request was simple enough, even though He could have bartered for her pitcher or waited for the disciples to return with one from the city. Surely, He was capable of getting water himself. But He asked for her hospitality. The code of hospitality had been handed down for generations. If someone asked for water and it was possible to grant the request, it was never denied.[3]

And yet, she hesitated.

Perhaps it was because of the white fringe on the hem of His robe. She knew He was a Jew without even having to ask, and Jews did not accept anything from the Samaritans. Not even water.[4]

There was a moment of indecision, a resistance to enter in. In that moment of pause, He turned the tables by offering a gift of His own. "If thou knewest the gift of God, and who it is that saith to thee, Give me to drink; thou wouldest have asked of him . . ." (John 4:10).

This surprised her even more. Surely, if He had known who she was, He never would have offered. She was a woman of Samaria, true. But she was the least of the Samaritans, despised by her own people. It was why she was at the unfrequented well at this time of day. She was not the upstanding woman He may have supposed her to be. What if He discovered who she was?[5]

What if He discovered who you are?

Would He still enter in?

"Go, call thy husband and come" (John 4:16).

She had no husband. And now He was entering into her pain, the place in her heart she held back, her place of shame.

But He didn't stop there.

He began to tell her story. A woman who had been married five times before. A woman now living with a man who was not her husband. It was the life she was shunned for.

He already knew.

He had known all along.

And still, He had chosen to enter into her story by asking for a drink, by offering her a gift. *A woman like her.*

But what was even more unexpected was what happened next. After she called Him a prophet, just after she whispered her hope in a Messiah to come, He told her who He really was: the Christ she had been waiting for.

"I that speak unto thee am he" (John 4:26).

The first clear announcement of who He was, a monumental moment in His ministry, was made to her: a single, rejected Samaritan woman standing at a well, in the heat of the day, on the outskirts of the city.

"And upon this came his disciples, and marveled that he talked with the woman" (John 4:27).

It wouldn't be the last time He would surprise them.

They would marvel again on a different day when He would boldly walk into a leper colony that others avoided at all costs. Why was it that He moved closer when others would turn in fear and disgust?

Jesus could have offered healing with words shouted from a distance or by simply waving His hand. But He didn't. On that day, when the leper came and knelt at His feet, He reached out His hand and touched him (see Mark 1:40–42).

He chose to heal an untouchable man with a tender touch.

When has He been tender with you?

The well on the outskirts and the outcasts from the leper colonies remind us that His love for people stretched beyond the boundaries of custom and expectation. Jesus sat down for lunch with the riffraff of society. The sinners. The criminals. The beggars. Anyone.

Everyone.

To the people on the outside, the invitation was clear: no matter the label, there is a place for you.

His work, the message of His life, His entire ministry, is people.

All of them.

If you've
traveled
alone to the well,

if you are
on the
outskirts
looking in,

lift up your heart.

He loves outside the lines.

The Places

JOHN 1; LUKE 19

It was Philip who first brought the news.

The One they had been waiting for had come. The One Moses and the other prophets had written about. *Nathanael, we have found him . . .* (see John 1:45).

Jesus of Nazareth.

But could it be true?

"Can there any good thing come out of Nazareth?" (John 1:46; emphasis added).

Nathanael wanted to believe. His heart wanted to match Philip's excitement. But it just didn't seem possible. The Messiah, a carpenter's son? From Nazareth? *It was such an ordinary place.* He couldn't help but hesitate because it just didn't make sense. Nathanael would have to see for himself. Philip didn't argue or try to explain.

He just gave a simple invitation, "Come and see" (John 1:46).

And so he did.

They were still a way off when Nathanael saw the man. There wasn't much about Him that was immediately impressive. But His first words *were* surprising, "Behold an Israelite indeed, in whom is no guile" (John 1:47). *What did that mean? The two had never even met.*

"Whence knowest thou me?" Nathanael asked (John 1:48).

Jesus answered, "Before that Philip called thee, when thou wast under the fig tree, I saw thee" (John 1:48).

Who was this man? And how did He know about the fig tree? Unless . . .

"Rabbi, thou art the Son of God; thou art the King of Israel" (John 1:49).

It may have seemed to anyone else like an exaggerated response. But not to Nathanael. Some sort of understanding had just taken place. Jesus knew what only Nathanael knew. That understanding burned a witness in his soul.

Is there something in your life only you and God would know?

It's such an unexpected place to meet the Messiah: under a fig tree.

Jesus smiled with understanding, "Because I said unto thee, I saw thee under the fig tree, believest thou?" Then His eyes lit up with anticipation, "Thou shalt see greater things than these" (John 1:50).

What were these greater things?

And where would they take place?

Nathanael was about to find out. The unexpectedness of the stable from thirty years before happened again under a fig tree, and that unexpectedness would continue—the extraordinary happening in ordinary places. Nathanael had no idea what was in store.

The sea would become more than just a spot for fishing. It would become a backdrop for raging storms to be stilled, for ships to sink with an impossible abundance of fish, for one man to step out of his boat onto the wind-whipped water and walk.

Graveyards would become places for rescuing the spiritually dead.

Colonies would become places of liberation where leprous captives would be set free.

Caves and sickbeds that would normally have

THE *Unexpected* DELIVERER

claimed their dead became instead memorials of the miraculous.

It wouldn't take long to realize that with Him hillsides could become holy, tax booths could house apostles, and wilderness places could become proving grounds of preparation.

This man would welcome the roads less traveled—roads that would take Him to ordinary people doing ordinary work in ordinary places. He would spend His ministry meeting individual people where they were, as they were. In *their* places.

It might seem unlikely for someone to meet so many individual people in so many particular places in three short years. But it wasn't unlikely for Him.

Where will He meet you?

He can find you anywhere.

Even in the top of a tree.

Chief tax collectors, rich men, are not the type of people who climb trees. Zacchaeus's reason for being up there was even more unexpected. He just wanted to see Jesus—even though tax collectors were not, by nature, accepted by those who were religious. Instead, they were traitors to the people. Thieves. Scoundrels. They aligned themselves with Rome—the enemy. Why would Zacchaeus be interested in a holy man?

And why would a holy man be interested in him?

When Zacchaeus arrived, the crowd was thick. He couldn't see Jesus over the press. The problem was, he was too short; perhaps that was what made him consider the tree (see Luke 19:3–4).

Do grown men climb trees?

That was where Jesus found him: in the branches of that sycamore tree. He called him by name, "Zacchaeus, make haste, and come down; for to day I must abide at thy house" (Luke 19:5).

What an unexpected place to meet the Messiah: in a sycamore tree.

Zacchaeus must have been shocked to be discovered there in the boughs of that tree and even more surprised that Jesus knew his name and that He would call him closer. Out of everyone in the crowd. Him. A tax collector.

The crowd was astonished that Jesus would choose to eat in a sinner's house.

The whole situation was out of the ordinary.

"But Zacchaeus made haste, and came down, and received him joyfully" (Luke 19:6).

It all began up in a sycamore tree. That was where Jesus found him, the same way He found Nathanael under his fig tree.

The same way He will find each of us.

Where is your tree?

When you find yourself in an
unlikely place, unseen,
there's still reason to *hope.*

You will be found.

The Miracles

JOHN 2; 11

The middle of His ministry was filled with mercy and miracles.

Mercy, defined as "especially active compassion" (Greek *Eleos*). *Miracles*, which became a beacon, a signature, evidence of who He was.

His very first miracle might seem inconsequential, perhaps even unnecessary to some. This beginning of miracles happened at a wedding feast. The need wasn't life-threatening or life-changing. The request was important only to her. His mother.

The beacon, the signature, the evidence from that beginning of miracles is clear—He will minister to the one. But there is more. On that night, in the middle of the wedding where they ran out of wine, there were six waterpots of stone that traditionally contained the water used for purification—the cleansing of hands, feet, and vessels. These were the pots Jesus asked the servants to fill with water to the brim. These were what He chose to use for the miracle.[6]

It was unexpected for more reasons than one.

Wine comes from grapes, not water—especially not washing water. But that was what He chose to work with.

After the miracle had taken place, when Jesus told them to draw out, the servants took a cup filled with water-turned-wine to the governor of the feast. He was astonished by the quality. He found it unexpected. Normally you serve the best wine first, but at this wedding the finest came last. It wasn't how things were done (see John 2:10).

What if the governor of the feast had discovered what only the servants knew, that the water meant for the washing of feet was what had been changed into the finest of wine? (see John 2:9).

The lesson is clear for those who are looking. What was about to happen over the next three years would transcend tradition, clash against culture, and unveil the unexpected. Jesus would change everything He touched.

Everything. Not only washing water to fine wine but also the likes of fishermen into faithful witnesses.

What will He make of you?

That least-to-best miracle from the wedding is sometimes viewed as foreshadowing—a reminder that Jesus would save His finest miracle for last. For three years from that wedding. For an Easter morning and a darkened tomb. But we're not at that part of the story yet.

First, there would be all the other miracles that came from not enough. Loaves and fishes multiplied. Multitudes filled. Baskets overflowing. But those three years of ministry would be made up of even more miracles that shouldn't have been, things the world deemed impossible. Inconceivable. Walking on water—that was unexpected. Cleansing blind eyes with spittle and clay—it hadn't been done before.

Men didn't walk on water.

The blind didn't see.

Lepers were healed, the lame would walk, a daughter would live again.

Those miracles became a backdrop to His true mission—the forgiving of sins, the redemption of souls. His was the healing of both physical and spiritual wounds.

His miracles would become a beacon, a signature, evidence of who He was.

Sometimes those miracles came soon.

But there were times when they didn't.

For the woman who waited twelve years after spending all she had, for the man at the pool of Bethesda who lay waiting next to the waters for thirty-eight years, and for Lazarus who lay dead in the tomb, the miracle came late.

For Lazarus, it seemed, too late.

When Martha, the sister of Lazarus, heard Jesus was coming, she went and met Him. "If you had been here," she wept, "my brother would not have died" (see John 11:20–21).

Why hadn't He come?

Even still, Martha believed in the unexpected miracle. She had seen it happen before. *Could it happen for her?* "I know, that even now, whatsoever thou wilt ask of God, God will give it thee" (John 11:22).

Even now.

Is it ever too late for the Lord?

"Believest thou . . . ?" He asked Martha. *Do you still believe even after the waiting? Even when it seems all is lost?*

Do you believe in who I am even with the stone in place? Am I still a God of mercy, even now?

Maybe those were the thoughts that filled her heart, and maybe that was why she responded, "Yea, Lord: I believe" (John 11:26–27).

"Take ye away the stone" (John 11:39).

They must have wondered what He was thinking, what He was doing. Who rolls away a stone from the final resting place of the dead? Then He cried with a loud voice, "Lazarus, come forth" (John 11:43). Come out of that dark place into the light. Come out of your sorrow and be healed.

And Lazarus did.

And so did Martha.

Jesus knew what He was doing all along. It wasn't too late. Comfort can come forth out of darkness. Healing can overcome. *Even now.*

And maybe you are still waiting.

For what should have been. For where you should have been. For how things should have been.

He is the beacon that draws the wounded heart in.

He is the especially active compassion.

The signature of promise.

The evidence that miracles still come.
Even after the waiting.

When things don't happen the way you want,
when you think it's *too late,*

remember:

*Darkness can't keep the light
from breaking through.*

The Entrance

MATTHEW 21

He rode in on a donkey.

If you were a country in bondage looking for deliverance from Rome, you probably wouldn't have thought it would come through a man in dusty robes riding a donkey. But Jesus came in through the Golden Gate of Jerusalem without a single weapon.

How would He set the people free?

It was such an ordinary animal, the donkey. It stood in stark contrast to a horse. It was a burden bearer, ridden by the humble people. Horses were owned by the wealthy and the Roman occupying army. They pulled chariots. They made up the cavalry.

Most of the people in Jerusalem, the ones praying for deliverance, would likely have believed that conquest over the Romans would require a noble steed and a sword.

Not one man riding in through the Golden Gate on a donkey.

But Jesus didn't come to overthrow the Romans.

This king came humbly, riding a donkey, bringing hope, healing, and heaven. It was unsought deliverance for many. Lackluster. Unless you were the man blind since birth. Or the woman sick for twelve years. Or the daughter of Jairus. Those were the people who understood the power of deliverance this man brought. They witnessed it firsthand, how He didn't always deliver in the way people might expect.

Where do you need His unexpected deliverance?

When Jesus entered in through the East Gate, clothes were thrown in His path—a royal carpet. Crowds gathered to cheer; they waved palms with shouts of celebration, and some people wondered why.

Hosanna! It was an ancient temple shout, reserved for festival days of jubilee. A reflective burst of joy in appreciation for the mighty works of God. *Hosanna is an exclamation of adoration.*

But hosanna is more than just adoration. Hosanna is a one-word prayer. Sometimes a one-word prayer is the most powerful kind. Help! Help me with my sin, help me with my burden, help me with my lack, help me with my doubt. *It is a plea for divine assistance.*

But hosanna is more than just a plea for help. Above all this, hosanna is a cry for salvation. Deliverance. Rescue. Relief. Redemption. Restoration. *Some things are bigger than Rome.* If people discovered that, if they realized what He was offering, perhaps their hosanna shout would shift to gratitude for what was to come.

Hosanna!

Adoration. A plea for help. A cry for salvation. Gratitude. Hosanna is allowing Him to do His work in His time, to offer deliverance in His way—even on a donkey.

If you had been in that crowd, which hosanna would you have shouted?

As the people of Jerusalem watched the triumphal entry taking place, they must have wondered why such an ordinary man was receiving such an extraordinary welcome. You hear it in the question that echoed through the crowd, "Who is this?" (Matthew 21:10).

Perhaps it was the woman who touched His robe, or the man who saw the great things, or the daughter He raised by the right hand, who answered in reverent awe, "*This is Jesus*" (Matthew 21:10–11).

Such knowing witnesses would lift their palm branches and join the joyful welcome, "Hosanna, blessed is he" (Matthew 21:9).

The unexpected deliverer. The burden bearer. The bringer of hosannas. A warrior fighting a different kind of war. A King ushering in a different kind of kingdom. A Messiah on a donkey.

This is Jesus.

When you are given a donkey
instead of a noble steed,
shout *hosanna!*

*He will still
give you reason
to rejoice.*

The Temple

MARK 11

It is Mark who bookends the moneychangers in the temple with the story of the withered fig tree.

Why?

That morning, Jesus was hungry. Seeing a fig tree with green leaves in the distance, He walked up to it hoping He would find something there, but He found nothing except the display of leaves. Nothing that would satisfy. Nothing that would fill. It was just a show. So, Jesus spoke to the tree and said, "No man eat fruit of thee hereafter for ever" (Mark 11:14).

What an unexpected thing to say to a fig tree.

When they arrived in Jerusalem, Jesus saw the temple in the distance, and perhaps He walked up to it hoping to find something there. But He found nothing except the display of those who sold and bought in the temple.

Nothing that would satisfy. Nothing that would fill. It was just a show. So, Jesus overthrew the tables of the moneychangers and the seats of the people selling doves, saying, "Is it not written, My house shall be called of all nations the house of prayer? but ye have made it a den of thieves" (Mark 11:17).

What an unexpected thing to do in a temple.

In the morning, the apostles passed by the fig tree again. Now it was all dried up, clear down to the roots. Peter couldn't help but make mention of the unexpected, "Master, behold, the fig tree which thou cursedst is withered away." It was almost as if He was asking, *How did you do that? In one night? And why?*

What was Jesus's reply? "Have faith in God" (Mark 11:21–22).

What an unexpected response.

It's like nothing we've seen from Jesus before. Turning over tables. Withering fig trees. It's improbable.

What is the lesson here?

Sometimes He turns things upside down.

Sometimes He takes things away that seem perfectly fine.

It's hard to understand why He might do that.

What does that have to do with faith in God?

Could the lesson date back to the time of Jeremiah from the Old Testament? It was a time when the people of Jerusalem were in a perpetual backslide, their hearts set on other things, a time when they refused to see the Lord. Jesus knew all about people refusing to recognize the Lord. In response to the people living in the time of Jeremiah, the Lord said, "There shall be no grapes on the vine, nor figs on the fig tree, and the leaf shall fade; *and the things that I have given them shall pass away from them*" (Jeremiah 8:13; emphasis added).

Trials come for different reasons. Sometimes God allows the trials inherent in mortality to touch our lives. Other trials come upon us because of someone else's agency. We often forget about a third reason for trials—trials that come because of our own choices. This was true for the people Jeremiah teaches us about. Their choices led to an unanticipated outcome. The Lord took the things He had given them away from them because they did not know Him, because they did not see Him there.

There was purpose in the taking away.

The taking away was meant to turn them to the One who can satisfy, the One who can fill. The taking away didn't mean all was lost. Jeremiah told them there would be a remedy for the hurt of the people.

There would be a balm in Gilead.

There was a physician there.

But they would have to find Him in that place.

Sometimes He removes the distractions so we can find Him in that place (see Jeremiah 16:17–21). Sometimes He turns things upside down. Sometimes He takes things away that we felt were perfectly fine.

Why?

To teach us to have faith in Him (see Jeremiah 9:23–24).

To lead us to the balm of Gilead (see Jeremiah 17:13–14).

To help us recognize the physician there (see Jeremiah 24:5–7).

"For I am with thee to save thee and to deliver thee, saith the Lord" (Jeremiah 15:20).

When the moneychangers left, the temple didn't stay empty. In the quiet reprieve, those who had been made to stay outside the gate Beautiful finally came in. "The blind and the lame came to him in the temple; and he healed them" (Matthew 21:14). In the quiet, they discovered the balm.

Healing isn't unexpected in His house.

It shouldn't be.

His is the house of answered prayers.

He is the One who satisfies. He is the One who fills.

Do you wonder if, after He was gone, the withered tree became a memorial for those apostles—a reminder that He came to heal, even if it meant turning things upside down or taking things away?

Even if it was unexpected.

When things are turned upside down
or things are taken away from you,
there is *purpose*.

Find the *balm* in Gilead.

Look for the physician there.

The Silence

It was a silent day in scripture.

During the last week of His life, on the third day before Passover, the Gospel writers seem to say nothing. On that Wednesday there were no recorded miracles, no healings, no teaching.

He was the Word, and there were none.

After the cursing of the fig tree, after the parables, after the great commandment. After the widow cast in her living, *all she had.* The day after He spoke to the apostles about leaving and then coming back again.

After that, there was silence.

For an entire day.

It was His last week.

Do you wonder if He was thinking about the leaving? The casting in all His living, giving His life? *All He had.*

Was He mustering strength?

Some people glance right over Wednesday; they move from the triumphal entry to the crucifixion without a second thought. Between the crowds and controversy, the silent day is forgotten. Should it be?

Maybe He was still teaching.

There is a message of stillness whispered through the pages of scripture, unexpected enough that you might miss it if you weren't searching for it. Quiet can be overlooked because it doesn't draw attention to itself, and yet we find great power there.

Still moments often precede a miracle.

When the Red Sea stood before them and the shouts of the army roared behind, in the moment when the cries of fear, the clash of swords, the fervor of battle would normally have prevailed, something unexpected took place. "Stand still," Moses counseled Israel, "and see the salvation of the Lord" (Exodus 14:13).

Stand still.

It happened again when Joshua led the people across

the river swollen over its banks. It wasn't until the feet of the priests stood in the waters of Jordan that the miracle came (see Joshua 3:15, 17).

Stand still.

It was advice given by her mother-in-law to Ruth, "Sit still, my daughter" (Ruth 3:18), and from a prophet to a future king, "Stand thou still a while" (1 Samuel 9:27).

Stand still.

And when Jehoshaphat gathered all of his kingdom in prayer before the temple, when the great multitude was coming against them in battle, when he cried to the Lord for help, the answer from the Spirit was clear: "The battle is not yours, but God's. . . . Ye shall not need to fight in this battle: set yourselves, stand ye still, and see the salvation of the Lord with you" (2 Chronicles 20:15, 17).

Stand still.

Jesus would have known about Moses, Joshua, Jehoshaphat, and Ruth because He was there. He would have known the promise from Isaiah, "For thus saith the Lord God, the Holy One of Israel . . . in quietness and in confidence shall be your strength" (Isaiah 30:15), because He was the One who spoke the words.

There was teaching in the stillness. In the silence. The quiet before the miracle.

It was true then. It is still true now.

The next day would bring the Passover meal. The betrayal of Judas. A blindfold, the cracking of a whip, a crown of thorns, a purple robe. The cock's crow. A trial. A crowd crying for crucifixion. The controversy. The cross.

"In quietness and in confidence shall be your strength."

We do not know what happened on the Wednesday of Holy Week. The scriptures are silent.

The scriptures are silent.

Still.

Perhaps there is a message there.

Sometimes the answer is no answer. Sometimes He is working in the waiting. Silent doesn't mean absent. He is there. Still.

Perhaps it is a lesson for facing our own dark days. When the multitude surrounds, when the battle rages, when we feel the urge to control the situation we are in with our own strength, our own plans, our own logic, in moments of greatest controversy, sometimes the answer from the Spirit is clear.

Stand still.

"In quietness and in confidence shall be your strength."

When your life is filled
with crowds and controversy, *be still.*

Let Him be the strength in the silence.

The Cross

JOHN 13; 19

On that last night in Egypt, every Israelite man took a lamb without blemish, a male.

They took the blood of that lamb and painted it on the two side posts and on the upper door post of the house. Then they burned the meat with fire and ate it with unleavened bread and with bitter herbs. "And the blood shall be to you for a token upon the houses where ye are: and when I see the blood, I will pass over you" (Exodus 12:3–13).

"And this day shall be unto you for a memorial; and ye shall keep it a feast . . . for ever" (Exodus 12:14).

Fourteen hundred years later, they were still keeping the feast of the Passover.

The celebration of deliverance.

On this particular Passover night, Jesus and His

apostles gathered together in the upper room to drink wine, to eat unleavened bread with bitter herbs, to keep the feast. All of the details were recorded by Matthew, Mark, Luke, and John, but not one of them mentions a lamb.

The firstborn. Without blemish. Whose blood would become a token.

Where was the lamb?

It was just the beginning of the unexpected deliverance Israel was about to experience.

After supper was over, Jesus girded Himself with a towel. Then He poured water into a basin and began to wash their sandaled feet fresh off the dusty road after the heat of the day. Usually the washing of feet was the job of the least in the household. It was the task no one wanted—the washing and the wiping clean from the mess.

So, when He rose from supper, and took a towel, and filled the basin, it would have been shocking.

Unexpected.

No wonder Peter started asking questions.

Because most people don't want to enter your mess. They don't want to touch your dirt. There are some places some people just don't want to go. Not Jesus. He wasn't afraid of the mess—He actually performed miracles with dirt.

There's nothing that would keep Him from entering in.

It was almost as if He were saying, "Don't keep your dirt from me, Peter. I know how to cleanse things. I will be tender with you. Gentle."

Let me.

It was an act of love. An object lesson before one of His best teachings, "A new commandment I give unto you, that ye love one another; as I have loved you, that ye also love one another" (John 13:34).

Will you let Him love you?

When He had finished, they went forth over the brook Cedron, and walked up a hill to the garden place Jesus loved to visit (see John 18:1). A place He had chosen to pray. But this was not just an ordinary prayer. This was a prayer of suffering.

Sore.

Exquisite.

Hard to bear.

A prayer that caused Him to tremble because of pain.

To bleed at every pore.

There was a moment when He wished He wouldn't have to drink the bitter cup, a moment when He considered shrinking. But He withstood; He finished the preparation. Blood was spilt, and through it protection would come (see D&C 19:15–19).

It began in a garden called Gethsemane.

That was where Judas found Him. There were a kiss and a sword and thirty pieces of silver, *and it had only been hours since His object lesson on love.*

And then, there was a cross.

It was Pilate who made sure a title was placed upon the wooden cross: "JESUS OF NAZARETH THE KING OF THE JEWS. . . . And it was written in Hebrew, and Greek, and Latin" (John 19:19–20).

As if His death was meant for all the world.

There was a crown of thorns. Nails in hands and feet. Vinegar. His mother stood by and watched. Her closest friends were there. There was a small group who provided stalwart support until the end.

Because that was what it was.

The end.

As that small group stood there at the base of that

wooden cross and listened to Him say, "It is finished" (John 19:30), do you think they wondered if it really was?

Standing under those dark clouds hanging low, with tears rolling down their cheeks unstoppable, do you think they felt defeat?

Failure.

Where was the deliverance?

"One of the soldiers with a spear pierced his side, and forthwith came there out blood and water" (John 19:34). The kingdom hadn't come. Even Jesus said it was finished. Over.

On the eve of the Sabbath, that small, stalwart crowd at the cross probably didn't realize that *finished* actually signified victory. Not defeat.

Accomplished.

Delivered.

The cross, known as the cruelest of deaths, the most demeaning way to die, a symbol of defeat, had unknowingly become a most unexpected means of deliverance for the people of God. They were people who should have known the story—how deliverance comes through the sacrifice of a firstborn lamb. *The Lamb.* Without blemish. Whose blood would become a token.

It came at the cost of great sacrifice. He descended below them all to accept the job no one wanted—the washing and wiping clean of the mess. To fulfill a role no one would volunteer for—no one but Him.

The unexpected deliverance became His greatest object lesson on love.

In coming days, many would recognize His gift of great love within the sacrifice, the token of His blood. Soon that defeated wooden cross would become a symbol of His victory.

What you view as defeat
can become His *victory*.
He came to
minister in the mess.

Let Him.

The Garden

JOHN 20

The morning began with her running to Peter and John to share a story of emptiness, tragedy, and abandonment.

When Peter and John took off running to see the empty tomb, it seems Mary Magdalene followed behind. They went inside and found the folded napkin and the other linen cloths, they saw how the tomb was empty, and then they went away again to their own homes.

But Mary stayed.

Weeping in the silence, she bent down to look into the tomb. She knew what she would find: emptiness. He was not there. In her grief and her sorrow, in her moment of greatest distress, He was absent. It was hard not to feel abandoned. Where had He gone? Where had they taken Him? Perhaps it was too much for her grieving heart to take in, because she turned away from the empty tomb.

We all have empty tombs.

There was a man standing nearby whom she didn't recognize. He asked why she was weeping. Maybe he could give her an answer. "Sir, if thou have borne him hence, tell me where thou hast laid him, and I will take him away" (John 20:15).

She supposed he was the gardener.

Just someone passing by on an errand.

Doing his work.

Expected.

Until He said her name.

And then, in that moment, everything was different.

Seconds before He spoke, Mary likely believed that death was final. The tomb had sealed off any other possibility. The circumstance was certain. Set in stone.

But now?

Now God was limitless. He could do things she never could have imagined: rolling away stones, filling the empty places with hope and with new possibility. Perhaps Mary had closed the book, but God was still writing the story.

If death isn't final, what else isn't either?

Sometimes we limit God. Sometimes we think that circumstances are set, that things will always be the way they are. Until someone rolls away the stone.

Sometimes God surprises us.

That was what happened for Mary. In the moment when Jesus said her name, Mary "turned herself" to Him (John 20:16). Then came healing over hurt, grace over grief, celebration over sorrow.

The morning began with her running to share a story of emptiness, tragedy, and abandonment. It was a morning that began with weeping and ended with her leaving the tomb to bear witness of the impossible.

That's the story God writes, the author and finisher of our faith. A story in which anything is possible.

Because our God is limitless.

Remember in moments that

cause us to *weep,*

when things feel set in stone,

we live in a

realm of miracles.

Anything is possible here.

The Message

JOHN 21

They went fishing.

After it was over, once things had settled down, they dusted off the old boat, climbed over the wooden side, and rowed out into the waters just the same way they had so many times before.

It had been three years since Jesus had first showed up on the shore. Three years filled with unexpected surprises and unanticipated wonder, events beyond imagination. But now, that life was over.

And this life, *this* was the life they knew.

They fished all night. When the morning came, they heard a call from the shore, asking if they had caught anything. They hadn't. "Cast the net on the right side of the ship, and ye shall find" (John 21:6).

It was probably seven and a half feet from where they

were currently fishing to the right side. *What were seven and a half feet in a sea this size?* But these men had learned to follow, so they did what the man on the shore suggested. It wasn't long before they were not able to lift the nets into the boat because there were so many fish.

These men had been in this situation before; they had spent an entire night with empty nets. All those years ago, they had cast the nets just where the unexpected man on the shore had told them to and found themselves sinking with the same kind of miracle.

They knew the man on the shore.

The disciples began the work of rowing in with the catch. But not Peter. He couldn't wait. He stepped onto the edge of the boat and dove into the water to swim.

Jesus was waiting there, standing on the same sort of beach where He had first found those same fishermen. He was making breakfast: fish grilling on the coals and warm bread, fresh baked and ready to eat. Jesus called to them to pull the heavy nets onto shore. Peter did as He asked and brought in the catch full of large fish. So many fish. The book of John records 153.

Someone counted the miracle.

"Come and dine," Jesus extended the invitation they

were so familiar with (John 21:12). *I've been expecting you. Come feast with me.*

There is a place for you here.

After they were finished eating, after they had time to rest and catch up, Jesus and Peter took a walk next to the net filled with 153 fish.

"Simon, son of Jonas, lovest thou me more than these?" (John 21:15).

Peter's answer was easy and expected. Jesus must have already known Peter would give the same answer he had given three years ago on the shore: "Yea, Lord." *Of course.* But this time, the invitation from Jesus was new.

"Feed my sheep" (John 21:16).

Peter was not a shepherd. He was a fisherman. He knew nothing about raising lambs. Perhaps that is why this very same exchange with Jesus happened two more times.

"Lovest thou me?"

"Feed my sheep."

It was a new call. Unexpected.

Three years ago, the task at hand had been to change a fisherman to a fisher of men. To teach him to find. To gather. To count. Now, Jesus was calling Peter to become a shepherd. To feed His flock. To care, protect, and love those who were brought in. There is no record of Peter raising sheep before.

But this was the work of Jesus, and now it was what Peter would do in His name.

The past three years had changed everything. The world would never be the same. And neither would Peter. He was no longer a fisherman. He would become a shepherd. The miracle of the Resurrection and the message of His grace were not meant to be kept in the upper room or on the shores of Galilee. This was no longer Jerusalem work.

"Go ye therefore, and teach all nations" (Matthew 28:19).

The kingdom had been inaugurated. The work had begun: a work that wouldn't be finished until the message—the good news—had gone forth into every nation, penetrated every continent, and sounded in every ear.[7] There would be persecution and pushback. But the miracles, the wonder, and the surprises would continue with a group of ruffians who had been raised up for this purpose.

Who would have imagined such a rough group would bring forth such a great cause?

The kingdom of God.

A doctor, a zealot, a tax collector, and a group of fishermen.

What a curious choice.

Such an inexperienced group.

But history shows that God loves qualifying the unqualified, equipping the unequipped, increasing the capacity of those who seem incapable. He did it for Peter and James, Nathanael and Mary Magdalene. And again for Paul, and Stephen, and Lydia, who would follow in their steps. The same way he would for an obscure boy of little consequence who would walk into a grove of trees almost two thousand years later.

He will do the same for you.

Look outside the boat. Just seven and a half feet. Right there, within your own circle of influence. There are miracles just waiting to be counted, his message waiting to be shared the way only you can.

"Behold I will send for many fishers, saith the Lord, and they shall fish them; and after I will send for many hunters, and they shall hunt them from every mountain, and from every hill and out of the holes of the rocks" (Jeremiah 16:16).

He is raising up a whole new group of ruffians.

Messy people magnified for His marvelous work.

The gathered doing the gathering, until the kingdom on earth becomes as it is in heaven.

Until Jesus Himself says the work is done.

If you feel like you don't match the message,

if the work feels *too great*

for the likes of you,

keep this in mind:

His ruffians will bring about the *restoration.*

It has always been so.

The End

REVELATION 21–22

There won't be a donkey.

On that day, the heavens will open, and there will be a white horse and a sword, just as you always imagined. The One who rides in on that horse will be clothed with a scarlet vesture, and He will be called Faithful and True (see Revelation 19:11–13).

Because He is true to His word.

Because He does what He says He will do.

Because He keeps His promise.

He will come, just as He said. On His robe will be "a name written, *KING OF KINGS AND LORD OF LORDS* . . . and they shall be His people, and God himself shall be with them" (Revelation 19:16, 21:3).

It will be a season of a thousand years, and Satan will

be bound, and the invitation will be sounded to every nation.

The welcoming in.

Come.

Gather yourselves together.

"And God shall wipe away all tears from their eyes; and there shall be no more death, neither sorrow, nor crying, neither shall there be any more pain" (Revelation 21:4). All of the hard things we've grown so used to—all of the painful things we know—taken away.

Because He is true and faithful.

Because He is true to His word.

Because He does what He said He would do.

Because He keeps His promises.

Even in unexpected ways. Even in unexpected situations.

He can be trusted.

We should have come to expect that by now.

This time when He comes, there will be a triumphal entry with a white horse and a sword. This time when He says it is finished, it will feel like a victory, the victory we have waited for. This time when He returns, the people will not need to ask who He is, they will know. *"I am*

Alpha and Omega, the beginning and the end" (Revelation 21:6).

And in the end, everything will be made right. In that city of celebration, there will be light, and the gates will not be shut—there will be a constant welcome. Because that is who He is. In that city of celebration, there will be no night, and no one will need a candle, because He is there and He will give them light.

And He will heal, and deliver again, and restore.

"These sayings are faithful and true" (Revelation 22:6).

Expected.

Because He is true to His word.

Because He does what He said He would do.

Because He keeps His promises.

And He promised to come.

"And the Spirit and the bride say, Come.

"And let him that heareth say, Come.

"And let Him that is athirst come" (Revelation 22:17).

And our hearts are so thirsty.

In that city there will be a pure river of water of life, clear as crystal, and on either side of the water the tree of life, and the leaves of the tree, for healing. "And whosoever will, let him take the water of life freely" (Revelation 22:17).

The Living Water.

It is something to look forward to.

Perhaps that is why He left us with His promise, *"Behold, I come quickly"* (Revelation 22:7).

Watch.

Be ready.

Prepare.

It is a promise to which He will be true: *"Behold, I come quickly"* (Revelation 22:12).

The white horse.

The sword.

The Deliverer.

A promise to which He will be faithful. *"Surely I come quickly"* (Revelation 22:20).

I am *true* to my word.

I do what I said I would do.

I keep my promises.

Just as you expected I would.

Even so, come, Lord Jesus.

Come.

Notes

1. See Alfred Edersheim, *The Life and Times of Jesus the Messiah*, 2 vols. (Grand Rapids, MI: World Publishing, 1971), 1:405–9.
2. See Edersheim, *Life and Times of Jesus*, 1:405–9.
3. See James E. Talmage, *Jesus the Christ* (Salt Lake City: Deseret Book, 1915, 1947), 173.
4. See Edersheim, *Life and Times of Jesus*, 1:405–9.
5. See Edersheim, *Life and Times of Jesus*, 1:405–9.
6. See Edersheim, *Life and Times of Jesus*, 1:357.
7. See Joseph Smith, *History of the Church of Jesus Christ of Latter-day Saints*, 7 vols. (1932–1951), 4:540.

Emily Belle Freeman is a best-selling author and popular inspirational speaker. She has a deep love of the scriptures, which comes from a desire to find their application in everyday life. She is the author of numerous books, including *Grace Where You Are, Creating a Christ-Centered Home; Closer to Christ;* and *Even This: Getting to the Place Where You Can Trust God with Anything.* She is a favorite speaker at Time Out for Women and a cohost with David Butler of *Don't Miss This,* a *Come, Follow Me* study channel on YouTube. Her greatest joy comes from spending time with her family. Read more at emilybellefreeman.com and follow Emily on Instagram and Facebook @emilybellefreeman.

Photo by Nikki Davis

David Butler's greatest love is people. He has adopted as a life motto: "Stuff no mattah, people mattah." His favorite people are his wife, Jenny, and their six darling children. Some of his other loves include good food, spontaneous adventures, Christmas morning, and the sea. David cohosts the popular YouTube scripture study channel *Don't Miss This* with Emily Belle Freeman and is the author of many religious books, including *Ites: An Illustrated Guide to the People in the Book of Mormon*; *The Peter Potential*; and *Almighty: How the Most Powerful Being in the Universe Is Also Your Loving Father*. Follow him on Instagram @mrdavebutler.